D0518390

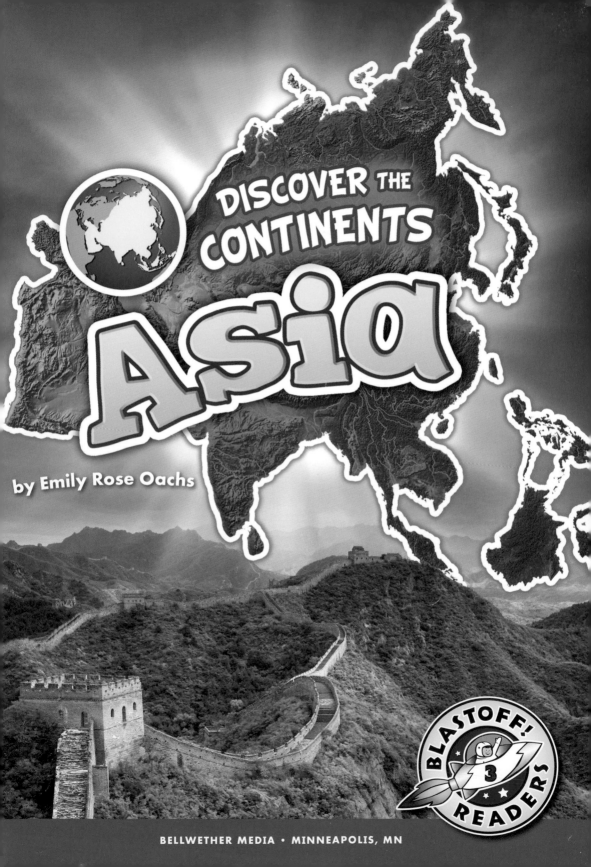

DISCOVER THE CONTINENTS

Asia

by Emily Rose Oachs

BLASTOFF!
3
READERS

BELLWETHER MEDIA · MINNEAPOLIS, MN

Note to Librarians, Teachers, and Parents:

Blastoff! Readers are carefully developed by literacy experts and combine standards-based content with developmentally appropriate text.

Level 1 provides the most support through repetition of high-frequency words, light text, predictable sentence patterns, and strong visual support.

Level 2 offers early readers a bit more challenge through varied simple sentences, increased text load, and less repetition of high-frequency words.

Level 3 advances early-fluent readers toward fluency through increased text and concept load, less reliance on visuals, longer sentences, and more literary language.

Level 4 builds reading stamina by providing more text per page, increased use of punctuation, greater variation in sentence patterns, and increasingly challenging vocabulary.

Level 5 encourages children to move from "learning to read" to "reading to learn" by providing even more text, varied writing styles, and less familiar topics.

Whichever book is right for your reader, Blastoff! Readers are the perfect books to build confidence and encourage a love of reading that will last a lifetime!

This edition first published in 2016 by Bellwether Media, Inc.

No part of this publication may be reproduced in whole or in part without written permission of the publisher. For information regarding permission, write to Bellwether Media, Inc., Attention: Permissions Department, 5357 Penn Avenue South, Minneapolis, MN 55419.

Library of Congress Cataloging-in-Publication Data

Oachs, Emily Rose.
  Asia / by Emily Rose Oachs.
    pages cm – (Blastoff! Readers: Discover the Continents)
  Includes bibliographical references and index.
  Summary: "Simple text and full-color photography introduce beginning readers to Asia. Developed by literacy experts for students in kindergarten through third grade"– Provided by publisher.
  Audience: Grades K-3.
  ISBN 978-1-62617-325-5 (hardcover : alk. paper)
  1. Asia–Juvenile literature. I. Title.
  DS5.O23 2016
  915–dc23
                        2015028681

Text copyright © 2016 by Bellwether Media, Inc. BLASTOFF! READERS and associated logos are trademarks and/or registered trademarks of Bellwether Media, Inc. SCHOLASTIC, CHILDREN'S PRESS, and associated logos are trademarks and/or registered trademarks of Scholastic Inc.

Printed in the United States of America, North Mankato, MN.

Table of Contents

The Largest Continent

Taj Mahal

Asia is the largest **continent**. It is almost five times bigger than the United States.

DID YOU KNOW?

- Asia is home to many places of religious importance. These include the city of Mecca and Jerusalem's Wailing Wall.

- Mandarin Chinese is the world's most common language.

- Earth's highest point, Mount Everest, is in Asia.

- Some of the world's first advanced societies began in Asia more than 6,000 years ago.

Mount Everest

Many people travel to Asia to see the Taj Mahal. This beautiful **monument** is in India. In China, the Great Wall winds across the land.

Where Is Asia?

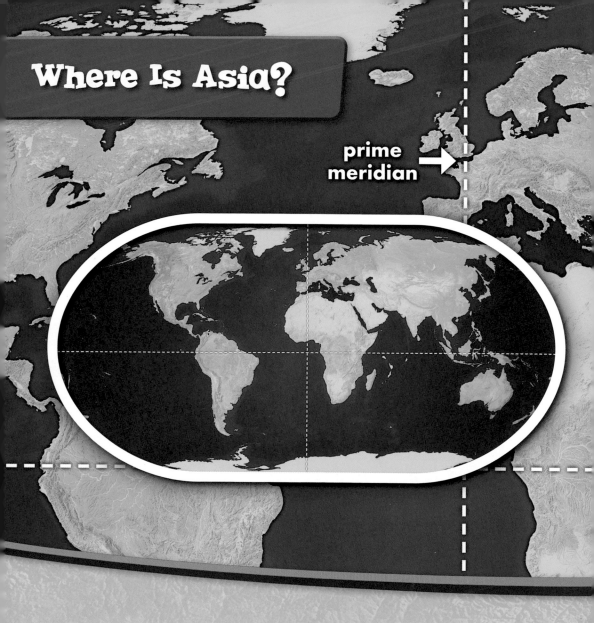

prime meridian

Most of Asia lies in the Eastern and Northern **hemispheres**. Some islands are below the **equator**.

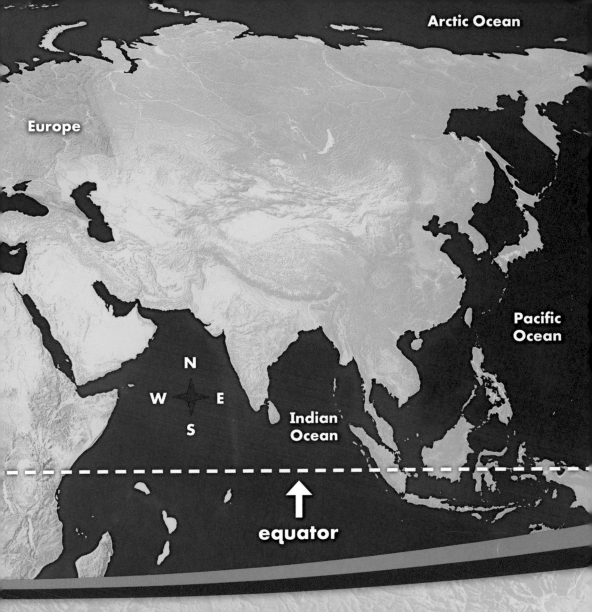

Europe borders western Asia.
To the north lies the Arctic Ocean.
The Pacific Ocean sits east of Asia.
To the south is the Indian Ocean.

The Land and Climate

Gobi Desert

Asia's huge size means its **climate** and land **vary** greatly. Northern Asia is bitterly cold. Sandy deserts cover southwestern and central Asia.

Rain forests grow in the south and southeast. **Tropical** islands lie off Asia's southern coast.

N
W E
S

Gobi Desert

Arabian Desert

Borneo rain forest

Sumatran rain forest

Borneo rain forest

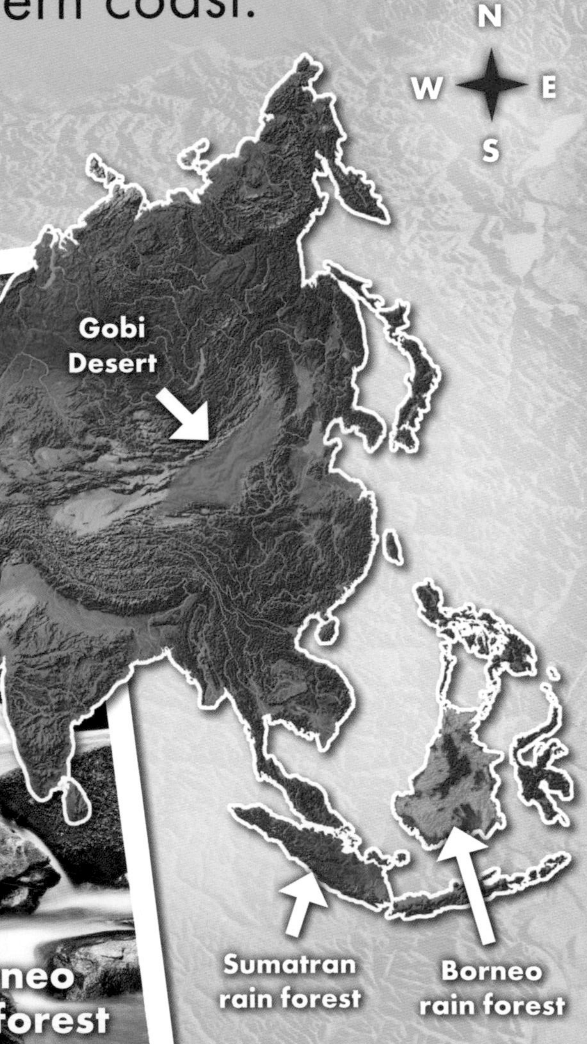

Many mountain chains cross Asia. The Ural Mountains form Asia's western border. The Himalayas include the world's tallest peaks.

Ural Mountains

Ural
Mountains

Himalayas

Himalayas

N
W • E
S

Coal hides beneath
Central Asia. Oil is
drawn from the land in
Saudi Arabia and Iran.

bamboo forest

saxaul tree

In eastern Asia, bamboo forests tower over the ground. Saxaul trees cling to life in the dry central deserts.

Birch and spruce trees grow in northern Asia. Rafflesia and orchids bloom in southeastern rain forests. In southern Asia, lotus flowers rise from lakes.

rafflesia

lotus flowers

Orangutans, giant pandas, and tigers are found only in Asia. In the north, polar bears, walruses, and reindeer brave the icy cold.

giant panda

polar bear

king cobra

tiger

Komodo dragon

In the southeast, scaly Komodo dragons hunt for food. King cobras slither through the rain forests there.

The People

Asia has 48 countries. Russia is the largest in size. It stretches across both Europe and Asia.

About 4.4 billion people call Asia home. No other continent has more people. More than half of the world's **population** lives in Asia.

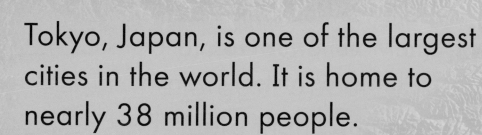

Tokyo, Japan, is one of the largest cities in the world. It is home to nearly 38 million people.

Each spring, cherry trees bloom across Japan. People hold **festivals** to honor the pink and white blossoms. They are **celebrations** of Asia's natural beauty.

Fast Facts About Asia

Size: 17,226,200 square miles (44,615,700 square kilometers); largest continent

Number of Countries: 48

Largest Country: Russia

Smallest Country: Maldives

Number of People: 4.4 billion people

Place with Most People: Tokyo, Japan

Top Natural Resources: coal, oil, wood, natural gas, iron, fish

Top Landmarks:
- Mount Everest (Nepal and China)
- Taj Mahal (India)
- Great Wall of China (China)
- Petra (Jordan)
- Burj Khalifa (United Arab Emirates)

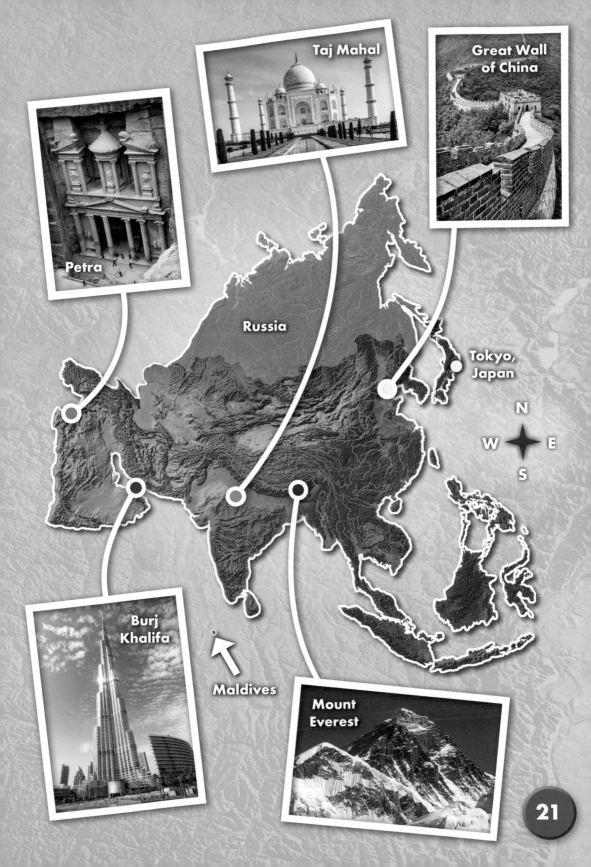

Taj Mahal

Great Wall
of China

Petra

Russia

Tokyo,
Japan

N
W E
S

Burj
Khalifa

Maldives

Mount
Everest

21

Glossary

celebrations—gatherings to honor and enjoy something special

climate—the weather patterns in an area over a long period of time

continent—one of the seven main land areas on Earth; the continents are Africa, Antarctica, Asia, Australia, Europe, North America, and South America.

equator—an imaginary line around the center of Earth; the equator divides the planet into a northern half and a southern half.

festivals—joyful events to honor special occasions

hemispheres—halves of the globe; the equator and prime meridian divide Earth into different hemispheres.

monument—a building that honors a person, place, or event

population—the number of people who live in an area

rain forests—thick, green forests that receive a lot of rain

tropical—part of the tropics; the tropics is a hot, rainy region near the equator.

vary—to have differences

To Learn More

AT THE LIBRARY

Demuth, Patricia Brennan. *Where Is the Great Wall?* New York, N.Y.: Grosset & Dunlap, 2015.

Williams, Marcia. *The Elephant's Friend and Other Tales from Ancient India.* Somerville, Mass.: Candlewick Press, 2012.

Zeiger, Jennifer. *Pandas.* New York, N.Y.: Children's Press, 2012.

ON THE WEB

Learning more about Asia is as easy as 1, 2, 3.

1. Go to www.factsurfer.com.

2. Enter "Asia" into the search box.

3. Click the "Surf" button and you will see a list of related web sites.

With factsurfer.com, finding more information is just a click away.

Index

The images in this book are reproduced through the courtesy of: feiyuezhangjie, front cover; Byelikova Oksana, p. 4; Zzvet, p. 5; F1 ONLINE/ SuperStock, p. 8; zodebala, p. 9; Potapov Igor Petrovich, p. 10; Olga Danylenko, p. 11; Pan Xunbin, p. 12 (top); Andrey N Bannov, p. 12 (bottom); Alexander Mazurkevich, p. 13 (top); XiXinXing, p. 13 (bottom); Eric Isselee, p. 14 (left); Hung Chung Chih, p. 14 (top right); La Nau de Fotografia, p. 14 (center right); A Periam Photography, p. 14 (bottom right); Erni, p. 15; Nikada, p. 16; Sean Pavone, p. 18; idmanjoe, p. 19; Aivolie, p. 21 (top left); turtix, p. 21 (top center); TonyV3112, p. 21 (top right); Konstantin Yolshin, p. 21 (bottom left); Yongyut Kumsri, p. 21 (bottom right).